First published in Great Britain in 2003 by
POETRY NOW
Remus House,
Coltsfoot Drive,
Peterborough, PE2 9JX
Telephone (01733) 898101
Fax (01733) 313524

All Rights Reserved

Copyright Contributors 2003

HB ISBN 0 75434 437 1
SB ISBN 0 75434 438 X

POPPIES IN THE BREEZE

Edited by

Heather Killingray

FOREWORD

Although we are a nation of poets we are accused of not reading poetry, or buying poetry books. After many years of listening to the incessant gripes of poetry publishers, I can only assume that the books they publish, in general, are books that most people do not want to read.

Poetry should not be obscure, introverted, and as cryptic as a crossword puzzle: it is the poet's duty to reach out and embrace the world.

The world owes the poet nothing and we should not be expected to dig and delve into a rambling discourse searching for some inner meaning.

The reason we write poetry (and almost all of us do) is because we want to communicate: an ideal; an idea; or a specific feeling. Poetry is as essential in communication, as a letter; a radio; a telephone, and the main criterion for selecting the poems in this anthology is very simple: they communicate.

CONTENTS

Poppies In The Breeze	Jan Maissen	1
The War To End All Wars	Joy Morton	2
World War II Cemetery, Jersey	Vera Morrill	3
The Confusion Of War	Paul Rand	4
Peace	Gemma King	5
Remembrance (An Unknown Soldier)	Nigel Gatiss	6
Nativity's Nightmare	David W Lankshear	7
I Believe In This Reality	Cathryn Harman	8
Who Is The Boss?	Paff	11
War - What Is It Good For?	Sarah Murkin	12
11th September 2021	Maria-Christina	13
Epiphany 2002	David Yarham	14
Feel The Peace	Joyce Dawn Willis	15
The Great War! 'To End Wars'...	Leslie Loader	16
Black And White	Mei Yuk Wong	17
Bosnian Homecoming	Joyce Walker	18
Tribute To The Lost Of America	Carol A Alvis	19
There Will Be Wars And Rumours Of Wars	Christine Nuttall	20
When War Commences	Barbara Tunstall	22
Unite	C A Keohane	23
The Duel	Mary Ratcliffe	24
The Shadow Of Evil	Colin Boynton	26
Time For War	Elaine Harris	27
Stories	Margaret Marston	28
No Fan Of War	Lorna Moffatt	29
'38, '39, '40	Robin Adara Lewis	30
Army Gratuity	Malcolm Williams	32
Farewell Century Of Tears	Robert Allen	33
No More War	John Gwynne	34
Bus Ride	Ruth Stern	35
Peace	Janet Howden	36
War And Children	Daniel C Wright	37
Glory	Gillian Browning	38

News Flash	Amy Claire Organ	39
Thought Of War	Heather Lynes	40
What Is It Worth?	Rachel Lamb	41
Dichotomy	S P Springthorpe	42
War	R O'Shaughnessy	43
America	Imelda Fitzsimons	44
War Is?	Nigel Lloyd Maltby	45
Born In Rebellion	Dorothy Brooks	46
Remembrance (1919)	Richard Young	47
Aid, First Or Last	J W W Griffiths	48
War On Peace	John Elias	49
Remembrance In The New Millennium	Michael Davidson	50
Curtain Call	Michael Fenton	51
America - The Tragedy	Benjamin Carr	52
Folly Of War	John Edney	53
Forgetting Her Feelings Forgetting Her Touch	Aled Hughes	54
Fly On The Wall	Michelle Landon	55
VE Day	Alex Laird	56
Vinegar And Brown Paper	Carolyn Garwes	57
Just Looking On	Sue Colson	58
Peace	Beryl L Lambert	59
Some Peaceful Alternatives	Elwyn Johnson	60
Living Humanity	Margaret Ann Wheatley	62
Living With The Enemy	Avril Ann Weryk	63
Is There Any Justice?	Ally Joyner & Andy McLaughlin	64
Railway Station In War	Arthur J Pullen	66
A Nation Mourns	C Worthington	67
Erased	M C Tshiamalenge	68
A Time For War?	Arthur Pickles	69
War	Jodie Booth	70
Beware Of War	James Rodger	71
Homecoming	Harold Wonham	72
The Soldier	Lydia Barnett	73
The Girl Who Kept Crying	Michael Wilson	74
The Concentration Camp	Ivor Percival	75

Poppy Day	Elliot Liversey	76
Islands	Thomas R Slater	77
1939-P45 (The Great Door)	Vann Scytere	78
For Those Who Came Home	Dale Mullock	79
The Harvest Of Conflict	Olga Margaret Moorhouse	80
Please Stop!	Phillip Lowe	81
Who Are The Dead	D Adams	82
Tomorrow?	D K Brough	83
Remembrance	Vicki Watson	84
The American Cemetery, Cambridge	Andrew Detheridge	85
Our Fathers Wha Faught Afore Us	Michael McLellan	86
War Has No Winners	Simon Icke	87
The Fields Of Flanders	Valerie Anderson	88
At The Feet Of Strand 22	Christopher David	90

POPPIES IN THE BREEZE
(For Dad - Harold Frowen)

The tension was high
as both men and boys alike
embarked on a mission
on that June 1944 night
they were prepared to fight
with all their might
so that you and I
may walk freely and in peace

They bade farewell to
loved ones and country
with tears in their eyes
and passion in their hearts
knowing they may never return
and with heavy hearts
they held their head high
proud to serve their country
in its hour of need

The memory of what had passed
that night and the years before
will never fade
and if you listen carefully
as the poppies sway gently in the breeze
you will hear the whispers
of those who fell saying
'Comrades tell the future generations
of what happened here
so that no more
will ever have to
fall'

Jan Maissen

THE WAR TO END ALL WARS

All around is
War.
A world dominated by
War.
Life is
War.

Life goes on
In the midst of war.
Working and eating and sleeping
In the midst of war.
Friendships grow
In the midst of war.

The friendships of war
Moulded in common experience;
The friendships of war
Strengthened in shared understanding;
The friendships of war
Survive even Death itself.

And Death is there
In the graveyard of war.
Side by side, friends die
In the graveyard of war.
Dying together, friendships transcend
The graveyard of war.

Joy Morton

WORLD WAR II CEMETERY, JERSEY

Wooden crosses silhouetted
Against a blaze of colour
Sons and sweethearts
Sleeping in serried rows
Unidentified,
Known only to God.

Flowers in profusion
Cushion our shocked senses,
Fail to conceal the wasted manhood
Reveal only
Spilled blood.

Our progress halted,
Emotions assaulted,
We wonder at each man's story
Reflect on war's dubious glory.

As the sentinel tower of bells
Chime out a requiem
We silently weep
And leave the young men
To their eternal sleep.

Vera Morrill

THE CONFUSION OF WAR

We haven't been asked,
If we were we'd say no!
The outcome's unknown,
And we don't hate the foe.

It doesn't arise
From chemicals or arms,
Nor does it concern
Unresolved moral qualms.

In spite of the spin
The message is clear,
It is not what they say:
'tis no 'war of merit'.

Paul Rand

PEACE

Peace is all around us,
Hanging in the air.
Sometimes we cannot see it,
But it is always there.

Whenever conflict rages,
Or war is going on,
There's always hope to keep us going,
Because peace has always won.

We say a little prayer sometimes,
For those who brought us harmony,
For those who died for the power of love,
And for those who brought us tranquillity.

And so we give our greatest thanks,
To those who have helped both man and beast,
For we have been given the greatest gift of all,
The gift of everlasting peace!

Gemma King

REMEMBRANCE (AN UNKNOWN SOLDIER)

And let it rain: give the world up to its tears.
The rivers that flow with blood, the product of our fears.
And find as we reclaim; so many souls in flames;
Each with a headstone granite formed:
To bear the etching of a name . . .
                                     Remembrances of the price we pay:
For playing our war games.

And death: where is its honour?
The feared heart so full of pain.
What glory in its banner; flown forlorn;
Or neatly folded on the cross;
Shredded, battle worn and torn.

And though their souls know freedom,
Whilst their bodies know the shame.
A billion unknown heroes; lie silent;
In the temporal halls of fame.
Remembered by their loved ones:
On trembling lips, a whispered name . . .
                                     'I never told her that I loved her.
Now it's too late:
I can't look into her eyes again.'

But death brings to each its own reward: beyond the hands of men.
Born to realms of spirit, love finds all, in the end.
To ask, when there is no question.
To shed love's tears, and not know why.
Maybe it's called redemption,
Or perhaps, 'it's just the way it is',
We live to love . . .
And then we die.

Nigel Gatiss

NATIVITY'S NIGHTMARE

Three fragments of newsprint drift,
Windblown, across the square.
One flutters briefly and a gunman
Empties his weapon at the movement.
The paper tattered collapses and dies
And the bullets ricochet off
The parking place of the pilgrims' buses.

The second sheet catches against
The body of a young woman.
She was betrothed, with child.
Now she is lying in the street.
As its editor has absorbed lies,
So the paper absorbs her blood
And clings to her dying face.

The last sheet rests against a doorway
In a shell-blasted wall
A sign beside the door swings drunkenly in the wind.
Proclaiming the building's passing purpose.
And yet, it still the rule of gun defies.
At the Church of the Nativity, here,
The grace of the Prince of Peace survives.

David W Lankshear

I BELIEVE IN THIS REALITY

A petty dust lies on a field of snow,
The allies' blood and that of men whose only hope was not to be there
And now they are not.

A plane flies and men scatter from it like birds away from their flock,
The night sky hides as well as hoped,
But the landing of the dead in their parachutes,
Is a sight not needed to raise the morale of the Yankee troops.

A sea of red water begins to rise to the shore,
It brings with it a debris of lives,

This is the year of 1950,
A year of peace,
As a man stands alone on French shores remembering the way it was -
The dead,
The sea,
The pain,
The German troops.

A woman bends over a gate to look at her child sitting on the
                                                             sandy ground,
   Naked and screaming,
They are both like this.

An old woman is awoken from her dreams and looks round in the dark,
She sees her husband being torn from their bed and taken into a lorry,
And her two teenage sons being taken into the road and shot,
She sees her youngest daughter scream as she watches this sight.

A man prays for his children,
He prays that what happened when he was a child should never
                                                             happen to them.

A soldier smiles as he looks at the photo of a now dead man,
The Führer stares out at him in black and white,
The soldier smiles because he knows the fury he fought is gone
                                                             but not at peace.

I stare at my grandfather,
And I am more proud than you can imagine,
I want to thank him for what he did,
For saving my mother,
For saving me.
I would like to ask him if he ever cried when he was there,
When he saw what he did.

A schoolboy stares at a book with vivid pictures and accounts,
But he does not understand,
What people risked for him,
He won't let himself let it in,
So they are just pictures and pages of words,
No matter if one of the men dead on the beaches,
On the minefields,
In the trenches could be his grandfather.
No matter because he is young,
Because he believes he is stronger than these men.

I look at medals; I look at stripes and stare as colours flood my eyes,
That is all they are,
All they ever can be to me -
I was not there -
I was not one of them,
I could never comprehend what these people went through to
                                        receive this honour,
The honour to live the way they want.

I stare at this -
This is not a poem and it is not a book,
It is a matter
And I wonder who has dealt with it the way it needs to be.

The death of thousands of men
(British or otherwise) for a cause that had no direct effect on them,
Was not glorious,
Was never great.
No war ever can be.

And above all it was not a mistake,
It simply was,
Maybe it shouldn't have been,
Or be again.

But that will not stop the memories of those who have lost,
That will not help the lost souls who could never rest in peace again.

I wonder if this will help anyone -
To understand.

To let it be more than words from the mouths of senile men.

Cathryn Harman

WHO IS THE BOSS?

In 'Most Secret War' WW2
MI5 wrote only what was true
He said he did not know
Who was his boss (page 243)
And neither did I know mine
Unless it was he, which it was
Such was total secrecy
But one thing was sure
It was not Hitler
He met his boss at Stalingrad and how
The end of all to be
Later Churchill rose in name
Adding to his trilby and cigar in fame
So the title of my little book became
'Churchill's Battle of the Beams'
No mistaking who was boss
But when it came to heavenly dreams
Infinity of space, satellites and beams
No one ever queries 'Who is Boss'
     God alone knows.
                            Amen.

Paff

WAR - WHAT IS IT GOOD FOR?

Global civil war
A war bred of ignorance
Incompetence, weak leadership
Too few willing to fight for change

A new era, the shutdown of the world
All nightmares cease
Reality gnaws through survivors existing
No easy road to wake up

Arid lands afloat as ships,
Ghostly screams echoing in the tide
Blood-red waste skirts the shore
Day gives way to eternal night

Gasping air from gloomy skies
Perishing monuments of past life
Still selfishly fighting one another
A world without end, but an end for us

Sarah Murkin

11TH SEPTEMBER 2021

I was with my mother,
on my way to school.
A plane roared overhead,
Mother stopped the car.

Then all was confusion -
the tall tower crashed down
with horrendous noise.
My mother held me close,
shielding me with her body.
A massive slab of masonry
crashed through the car roof
hitting Mother on her head,
and she lay still.

We are exhorted -
'Forgive your enemies,
bless your persecutors.'
But how?

Our faceless enemy
killed himself.
But ultimately -
who was to blame?

Avenge my mother I cannot.
I ask God to help me.
May God forgive you,
whoever you are.
For I cannot . . .

Maria-Christina

EPIPHANY 2002

By the time the Magi came
the decorations had been taken down,
the tree untrimmed, the baubles packed away.

Twilight gave way to starlight as they came:
Saturn was bright among the Hyades
and Jupiter from Gemini looked down.

Strange gifts they brought and urgent questioning:
'Where is the king whose birth you celebrate?'
We did not know. Our Christmas junketing
had scarcely left us time to think of him.

Gold as a present they had brought for him;
'A gift,' they murmured, *'worthy of a king,'*
and we agreed. Their other gifts, we thought,
were less appropriate. Incense and myrrh
bore overtones of worship and of death.
The first we'd left behind in Sunday school
and of the second seldom cared to think.

Their questions and their gifts disturbed us.
The king they sought we viewed with some unease.
Eager, we'd been, to celebrate his birth,
much less so to accept his sovereignty.
To *'love our neighbours as we loved ourselves'*,
his firm command, we'd found too difficult.

'Go home,' we urged them, *'by another way.*
The world is little changed since last you came.
Still Herod's hand is red in Bethlehem
and still for murdered children Rachel weeps.'

David Yarham

FEEL THE PEACE

Without the terrible horror of wars,
would we experience the tranquillity of peace?
Do we take the peaceful serenity for granted,
until one day it quite suddenly does cease?

Without storms and icy-cold winter's bareness,
would we appreciate the glow of summer and spring?
The joyful laughter of our children,
whose happy hearts at play, take wing.
Dells of snowdrops, the bluebell woods,
and fields of poppies dancing so merrily.
Golden sunshine and peaceful blue skies,
with the birds singing in sweet harmony.

Joyce Dawn Willis

THE GREAT WAR!
'TO END WARS' THAT IS WHAT THEY SAID!
YES THEY DID!

One would think that a War that was *great*,
Would have taught us a thing or two,
To stop such nonsense behaviour,
From just happening again, *wouldn't you?*
But *no*, we just carried on,
As though nothing, abnormal, had happened.
Wars, you see, are to so many, *just normal*,
So in time another War 'just happened',
Wars, just sort of, to so many,
They just come 'out of the blue'
Yes! To so many, just 'out of the blue'!

There is . . . to so many . . . no way to stop them,
They just happen,
They just come 'out of the blue'.

You see when the *Great War* was over,
There was lots of rejoicing and fun,
As most got back to self and the wife,
So nothing was done to make certain,
That a War wouldn't just happen again.
But it did, during a morning,
When marching, I was, in the Hampshires,
To fill sandbags,
In Southampton's New Docks,
Next to the Royal Pier.
It was a Sunday morning,
I remember we all gave a cheer,
As we continued our march,
Now with a jaunt,
To fill sandbags, in the New Docks,
That are next to Southampton's Royal Pier.

Leslie Loader

BLACK AND WHITE

To take either black or white
is an easy way
no similarity
but differences

You are either black minority
or white majority
no compromise
but discrimination

To take side
to stand for your principal colour
but don't forget
in between black and white
there is g-r-e-y

I am neither black nor white
but yellow

Mei Yuk Wong

BOSNIAN HOMECOMING

We have come home, the lucky ones
Whose houses have not been bombed,
Comfort friends with only burnt out shells.

We cannot make them tea, the kitchen sink
Is full of crap and stinks. A soldier's calling card,
His way of telling us we're s**t.
There's no mains water, cleaning up will take forever.

Our clothes are here, hanging neatly on the rails.
Not a good sign, sometimes they leave explosives
In the pockets. One of our neighbours lost a hand.

The garden's overgrown, the grass waist high,
But still I see the patch of ground, the shallow grave,
The day they tied my father's hands,
My mother being dragged against her will.

Face down on the floor, a gun to my head,
While she kicked and screamed and finally submitted.

Then came the gunshots, the silence.

Before we fled, we buried my father's body in the garden,
This garden, where he stood helpless,
Watching while they raped my mother.
The bullets must have come as a relief.

I pick wild poppies, lay them at his feet,
Try to remember we are the lucky ones.

Joyce Walker

TRIBUTE TO THE LOST OF AMERICA

Luke a huge bird swooping on its prey
It skims through the air with immaculate timing
On its unseeing and innocent victims,
Adversaries to its thinking.

So many caught unawares
Going about their daily business,
Totally oblivious to their ensuing fate,
Not for one moment imagining they would
Be caught up in such an horrific plight.

Time stood still for those, whilst many
Marked time in anticipation of news,
Hoping, praying, questioning, waiting
For news - good or bad - but oh to know the truth!

Lives lost for what?
To prove a point? To seek revenge?
History in the making and the breaking.
We, at home, can merely watch and wait,
Only imagining the trauma and the devastation.

Carol A Alvis

THERE WILL BE WARS AND RUMOURS OF WARS

They take their chance
In harsh terrain;
But well they know,
There's little gain,
Where violent gun
Is master here,
And daily life
Is masked with fear.

They take their chance,
We knew they would,
They feel they're doing
What they should.
Among the crumbling buildings, hide
A danger that spreads far and wide.

They take their chance,
We've sent them out,
Our brave marines
And troops, no doubt,
A medal here, a medal there
And back to normal, as it were.

They take their chance,
There is no doubt,
They know what war
Is all about.
But who has thought,
The damage done
Is buried deep,
In these, our sons.

They take their chance,
We send them home,
We pat their backs
And praise their names,
But they will never
Be the same.

Now this new war,
And these new men,
Will suffer at war's hands
again.

Christine Nuttall

WHEN WAR COMMENCES

An act of aggression made to mankind
Cannot be left unpaid
A debt is owed someone must pay
Retribution will be made

How can they do this for what reasons
People happy a zest for life suddenly gone
No goodbyes or loving words wickedly destroyed
Leaving their devastated loved ones in a deep dark void

What kind of humans could do this to another
No seed of love could reproduce to make father and a mother
What are we up against, what will we see
No mercy or compassion just evil idolatry

Though sadly a war is looming it may be very near
Bringing pain and devastation lost hope and fear
Most victims could be innocent the choice is never theirs
Nowhere to run and hide themselves who cares

Visions of horror loved ones hurt or dead
Read about daily too traumatic to be said
When the last world war was fought
It was to end all wars so we were told
But this time the aftermath
May curse the very bold

Dictators who are evil and only worship power
They hope a war will be their finest hour
Who would believe such madness exists
Get rid of them soon before they are missed

War will come to destroy the evil one
There is no gain but justice must be done
God gives life it is his right to take
so who is the infidel killing for hatred's sake

Barbara Tunstall

UNITE

Now is the time to unite nations
Of all creeds and languages.
Now is the time to make peace
And leave behind jealousy.

This is the time to make love
And forget about hate and war.
This is the time to negotiate
And understand one another.

Now is the time to end destruction
And build a new world for our children.
Now, is the time to make love,
And forget about the evil war.

C A Keohane

THE DUEL

Beyond our comprehension.
Destruction born of hate.
Twin towers yielded helplessly . . .
    their terrifying fate.
The world observed in horror.
Lives expunged by murder,
that changed the course of history
and altered life forever.
Vengeance was the first response.
The cry for war was dominant.
An 'eye for an eye' . . . the battle cry.
Death to Bin Laden imminent.
As the haunting scene unfurled
'minds' paused to think again.
Afghans were starving . . . dying
in their bleak austere terrain.
Poverty claimed a million lives
as people fed on grass.
No hope. No homes. No sustenance.
Impenetrating impasse.
Countries forged a common bond
to ride the world of terror.
Others changed: Holy War,
    'Jihad to America'.
As New York grieves and mourns the dead,
the world reflects upon the cause;
to question why such hatred burns
defying consequence and laws?
A dual response has now evolved
to terminate the terror
and feed the starving multitudes
caught up in abject horror.

And so we seek a dawn of hope,
that no one died in vain.
For them, respect and honour
to release the world from pain.
To understand each country's need.
To vanquish war and strife.
To feed the children of the world
and revere the right to life.

Mary Ratcliffe

THE SHADOW OF EVIL
(13th October 2002, may the souls of Bali rest in peace)

For all those souls who died in fear
May you find peace at last,
No more to run, no more to hide
Your hurting now be passed,
And as the terror spreads its wings
And flies across the land,
Those of you who wait with tears
Can only watch and stand,
Not knowing where the shadow is
Or where it next may call,
Together standing side by side
Together standing tall,
All as one in grief and pain
Yet feeling all alone,
The whole world looks on in shock
For those not going home,
Tomorrow is another day
One we all must face,
Not knowing what the future brings
For the human race,
Together we must stand up
Strong and proud and tall,
Fighting back together
Until the shadows fall,
And when at last that day is here
When the world is free,
No more souls need die in fear
Perhaps we all will see,
That all it really takes is love
And just a little care,
To live our lives in harmony
The world is ours to share.

Colin Boynton

TIME FOR WAR

This time
There will not be
Any war cemeteries
Nowhere left to dig
Nothing left to put in the holes anyway
Nobody left
Nobody

Please make a little room for us
Shades of Hiroshima

Elaine Harris

STORIES

When I was small he told me stories of
Wars and battles and all that stuff
But I was too young to understand
About soldiers, battles and big brass bands

When he was old he sat in a chair
He told me stories about how brave they were
I listened in silence and soaked it up
I wanted to learn I couldn't hear enough

I wanted to piece it all in place
What caused these wars and the disgrace
The struggle for power that men
Sent soldiers into battle again and again

We can learn a lot from books
About heroes and important dukes
But better to hear from the grass roots
The men who marched in big heavy boots

Margaret Marston

NO FAN OF WAR

Tell me this
And tell me no more:
How exactly
Do you define *war?*
Is it 'ethnic cleansing'
As the Slavonics claim?
Or just bloody murder
In a despot's name?

Twelve disciples of the devil
Always live here on earth:
To start their wars
And give their master yet his mirth.
So is their war just
A party game from out of hell
Or do they try each generation
Giving us the death knell?

Ordinary people, on this earth,
Like you and me
Must learn to deny these devils
And clearly see:
Everyone is entitled to their own land,
Home and ware
And the name they give their god
Is entirely their affair.

Lorna Moffatt

'38, '39, '40

We tramped weald and down,
rolling green under clear blue.
Post-school spirits up,
enthusiasm fired
on fresh air, freedom was all,
cutting crisp and silken-shot.

Dawn. Up like a shot,
tents down,
gear stashed. All
raring to march into the blue
of a new day, fired
by a sun on the up.

Herr Hitler's time up,
politicians' eyes bloodshot,
rhetorical broadsides fired,
ultimatums down.
Wireless, out of the blue:
' . . . we are now at war . . . ' Is that all?

Varsity boys, all
four of us signed up
for the lighter blue.
We'd give it our best shot -
bringing Hitler down.
In France, first salvoes fired.

Props turned, engines fired.
Training-fresh, all
scrambled in a daze, youthful down
on chins. Kites roaring up, up -
ducklings line astern, shot
at and firing into tracered blue.

And out of that lethal blue,
reserve tank and cockpit fired
by one last silent shell-shot,
I spiral, fall. All
earth, sky and flames scrambled up,
Blue Four going down.

Blue. All
fired up.
Shot down.

Robin Adara Lewis

ARMY GRATUITY

A medical discharge from the regiment
he refuses to quit; from high-hazard career
to low-risk languishing. So he goes
to sea during squalls, land legs alien
on deck, new yacht sails snorting
the wind like a fix of coke.

Without angst, his harbour woman monitors him
in Cardigan Bay, safely griddling Welsh cakes.
In private, she admires the military medals
secreted in a Havana cigar box.
At last, her hero returns to her each night.
Maybe she can shed the dread of their
son growing up - signing up.
Perhaps she can even get married now?

The veteran's nightmare is always the moment
he lobbed a grenade into a terrorist cave.
He still smells the hatred of the surviving zealot
he carried out to paramedics. That boy
was younger than his son, rags and limbs red.
No name; no surrender; electing to be dead!

Malcolm Williams

FAREWELL CENTURY OF TEARS

Ring out the old century.
Ring the bells with vigour and joy.
Farewell the black years,
century of massacres, folly and tears.

Ring out the century of fears.
Close the unclosed eyes
of wasted, sacrificed youth
in fields clothed in blood.

Ring out the century of cares.
Earth weeps with morning dew
the hunted white man,
black man and Jew.

Welcome a new dawn
when humanity
discards inhumanity.
Worthy to clasp the hand of its God.

Robert Allen

No More War

The common people want to see
stability in the Middle East,
to see them live without a war
and enjoy a lasting peace.

But politicians think differently
George Bush and Tony Blair,
they want to now kick Saddam's butt
as long as they're not there.

These puppets don't do the fighting
they leave it to the men,
to do their bidding for them.
Their hands don't get dirty then.

But the call of the British people
say no to another war,
we don't want our sons dead or maimed
not ever, not anymore.

John Gwynne

BUS RIDE
(Jerusalem Tel-Aviv Line. Bus No 480)

After the No 18 bus bombing
After the forest was set alight
I'm back on the road on a 48 bus
one of 50 pairs of passenger-eyes
    travelling in trust
for 45 minutes, aliens or allies
passing the dying tree trunks. Reluctant eyes
avoid the blackened hillside.
    Naked rocks
like a skin suffering the deadly pox
shun the sniping winter rays
criss-crossing interchanging ways
    slanting shadows
on the road signs.

    I wonder who
might hold a gun, you
    or even you,
in a mantle of ignorant innocence,
    or who
would hide a bomb
in this moving bus,
surely not one of us
    on a sunny winter morning?

Ruth Stern

PEACE

Love is everywhere,
love is all around,
it really isn't difficult,
for true love to be found.
If only all the countries,
in the world with bombs and guns,
would take a look around them,
and see their ways are wrong,
then maybe they would find love,
and all the guns would cease,
and once again we all would live,
in a world of love and peace.

Janet Howden

WAR AND CHILDREN

The guns fire,
The missiles fly,
And there they stand,
Directly in front,
Yet oblivious to what is going on,
Not knowing what's happening,
Not knowing what will happen.

Their land,
Their playgrounds,
Their fields,
Being fought over,
Being scrapped over,
Being killed over,
Yet they don't want this,
All they want is to be happy and play.

Things being fought over,
By people they don't know,
Being scrapped over,
By people they don't know,
Being killed over,
By people they don't know,
But wait, if only for a second,
They, are children.

Daniel C Wright

GLORY

The fight goes on,
not for the glory
or for what is right.
The focus lost
to all who join
so futile in its might.
Flip a coin
to find out
who the victors be.
No you, not him, not me.

Bury me in soft brown earth,
write about me what I'm worth.
Sing my glory in a song
the other side was in the wrong.
He was buried with his gun
his own glory also sung.
Who was right, when all along
we were both victims of the masters,
mapping out our life disasters?

Gillian Browning

NEWS FLASH

The President announced
Today
Another war.
Another fight without cause,
another battle without reason
We will fight terrorism
and the imprisonment of innocents.
We will kill more innocents
and ravage more land.
We the allied good
will fight the band of evil.
We the allied soldiers
will kill a band of brothers.

Trust me when I say

This war is a last resort
to a battle of wills.
This war is the first strike
to a never-ending battle.
Listen, this war will protect your children
from the evil of our enemy.
Listen, this war will kill your husbands
and leave your children fatherless
Our future is safe and free
We will destroy this evil forever.
Our future is the past repeated
We will war again.

Amy Claire Organ

THOUGHT OF WAR

Just stop for a moment, think and reflect.
Do we need to listen with fear, this talk of war retouched?
Can't we stay a green and pleasant land?

Should our brave soldiers, our would be brave warriors,
Slip and slide in the shifting sand.
We should stand together and be mindful,
Of the misery and destruction war would bring.

On both sides of this equation, innocent lives will be lost,
Never again shall we hear fathers and sons chatter and sing.
Is this trodden path the only avenue to pursue?

Can't we stretch out our hands in a gesture of peace,
To rescue our world from this scourge, this menacing presence?
To leave a legacy to the next generation.
Enable them to linger in an English rose garden, to savour the essence.

Heather Lynes

WHAT IS IT WORTH?

Emphasis upon what is worth nothing
Pressure on what we value not
Is it worth the fight, the blood of another
Upon your hands when you did not shed a single drop?

People's lives are more valuable and delicate than winning land
Or a battle
So why is it that we lust for the lower option?
We choose to spear a person rather than spare them
Love and feelings are more than a notion.

We need to create a world of peace and not of blood-stained land
Where the angels sing at every day's birth and never stop even
At its dusk.
A world of happiness and purity rather than the devil's mark
Upon every hand.
Why is the evil one a part of our haven? He deserves not even
An elephants tusk.

So God grace this land with your helping hand that brings
Love and beauty
Don't let him win because hell will come if you turn your back
Light not dark
White not black

Help us now!

Rachel Lamb

DICHOTOMY

These people make an appointment for the beginning
A calendar date in red. They know little else.

Their flowers are poppies
The bread knife a bayonet
Their water carriers are helmets
The fruit - overripe hand grenades.
A house for the hospital
The basement, a shelter
The car, a tank and the garden, a graveyard -

But the corpse is dead,
And dead only.

S P Springthorpe

WAR

From Genghis Khan who sacked Rome,
To Montgomery, and the dastardly Saddam Hussein,
Who bombed the Kurdish city of Halabja,
With cyanide bombs, and those with limbs missing,
And cancers roam the city to this day,
With no medical treatment at all.

Man is the only animal
Who systematically sets out
To destroy his fellow species.
All the dead of all wars,
Will curse in their graves,
Especially those of the twentieth century -
Two and a half million dead - young men,
British youth, in the first war -
They indict Haig who was their commander.

R O'Shaughnessy

AMERICA

On the eleventh of September 2001
The world stood still for what has become
A moment of madness for all to see
With death and destruction and eternity.

Those men of madness in flight took hold
Showing just how vulnerable if truth be told
That security can lapse in our hour of need
As terrorists reign when they plant their seed.

For thousands of people it was just another day
In offices, on planes, in school, or holiday
Until that moment when the world as one
Was aghast with horror at the awful deed done.

Thousands were trapped, some still in pain
As they tried to overcome the terrorists in a plane
While others could do nothing but sit and wait
Or phone relatives and accept their fate.

The world sat still as the news was read
Many bodies buried as the cry for aid
Was answered by firemen who just didn't know
The end was near for they couldn't say no.

America with riches - they've got it made
But can't do a thing, while those lie dead
Under the rubble of burning and stone
Building those tower blocks that stand alone.

And more innocent lives will be lost no doubt
For it's hard to keep those evil men out
While poor individuals mourn their dead
As the terrorists always seem one step ahead.

Imelda Fitzsimons

WAR IS?

Wanton
Annihilation
Rebounds

Revenging
Evil
Slaughter,
Obliterating
Life,
Violating
Endless
Souls.

Nihilism
Overpowers
Truth,
Humiliates
Innocence,
Nullifies
Graciousness.

Nigel Lloyd Maltby

BORN IN REBELLION

Born in rebellion are the sons of men.
Nation sets her face against the nations,
rising sons of men.
Far better is the day you die
than the day you're born.
When peace came forth into the world,
you turned to face the storm
and put to death in rebellion
Jesus Son of God,
by the sons of men He made!
Better that they dwell with their brothers
in the silence of the grave.
Is there any way out,
is there any escape,
from the darkness and the sword,
and betrayal's trusted fingers,
that makes our hopes ignored?
For deep within the heart of men,
a rebel spirit lies,
and rises up in anger,
like smoke that fills your eyes.

Dorothy Brooks

REMEMBRANCE (1919)

The guns have fallen silent
And the people can rejoice,
But who is there to speak out;
Who will lend a voice
To the millions of young people,
The fallen of each side,
Sacrifices on the altar
Of nationalistic pride?
They did not pause to question:
They did not count the cost;
They went where others sent them;
To the legion of the lost.
For them, no quiet churchyard:
They were buried where they fell;
They, whose path to Heaven led them
Through the bloody jaws of Hell.
At Paschendaelle and Ypres: *(Pronounce as 'Wipers')*
On the Somme or at Arras; *(Pronounce as 'Arrass')*
Whether beaten down by bullets
Or slowly choked by gas,
They gave up their tomorrow
To build a better one for us,
So when the trumpet sounds 'Last Post',
Don't ask, 'What's all the fuss?'
The least that we can do for them,
Or else they died in vain,
Is to remember what they did for us
And to vow, 'Never again!'

Richard Young

AID, FIRST OR LAST

I've often thought it funny,
now think it even more,
while we send aid to poorer nations,
there are those that send them war,
tanks and missiles are no good,
there must be some mistake,
you can't eat tanks or missiles,
someone must be on the 'take'.

It seems half the world is now at war,
and there are those that fan the flames,
to gain control of the poorer nations
must be their only aims,
lets hope the aid that *we* send,
will reach them very soon,
before the 'tanks and missiles',
they only lead to gloom.

J W W Griffiths

WAR ON PEACE

Last night I lay a-sleeping, I dreamed a dream so rare
I stood in old Jerusalem besides the temple there
I heard no children singing nor angel voices speak - but
screaming shells and bombing and then the people weep
The temple walls like Jericho's were reduced to rubble, dust
and tanks once merciless in death untracked and turned to rust
The houses, homes once filled with love
Laid waste on every hand, with children maimed and parentless
Through the intransigence of man.

Beloved names like Bethlehem, like Hebron, Galilee
Were battle wrecked and bloodstained as was Gethsemane.

Young people wrapped in dynamite
Persuaded by their creed that martyrdom in paradise was theirs
if others bleed
God, what a loss and what a price to pay by one so brave
And what abomination would send young zealots to such graves
For wherever rabid war is raged and shells and bullets fly,
it seems to be the *innocent* that are always first to die

John Elias

REMEMBRANCE IN THE NEW MILLENNIUM

From hell they came in tattered uniforms
To lands which hailed them warriors
While those at home
With such authority as time allowed
Spoke words of epic tone
As actors on a vast and unseen stage.

To those
Who bore their pains without complaint
And those
Who lived their lives with empty hearts
Scant regard was given.

Now we,
Though fettered time gave rise to guilt,
See those whose lives
No longer buy much needed time
Engage in conflicts we had sought to end.

We must not lose our hopes,
Naked as they are,
Forswear beliefs, deny that love
The world has found so hard to give.

Michael Davidson

CURTAIN CALL

The opera continues,
the heroes sung home:
blood dries as fast
as memory fades.

The curtains fell,
and fall.
Leaders bow
to the applause;
breathing in,
with nostrils flared,

the stench of recognition.
In Memoriam

Michael Fenton

AMERICA - THE TRAGEDY

MTV madness swept saints into huge wasted piles, there roasted tortured and blown into oblivion's breath with screams and wailing sirens failing falling streets of tears and terror, on beat camera filming faces crying a thriller snaking out of the pitiful thirty-five millimetre where watchers bathed in the blood of those once human, now tortured by the hot light and trapped in a pen made up with shrapnel from the rotten earth covered face acting within dead limbs of a rotting country rolled up and smoked in a commercial hash of media mayhem once tasting sweet and simple but tongue twisted black suits swept along by the lens let it burn itself into towering memories thrown to the winds the dust swirling above the lifeless puppets no strings detached real life drama wired into our red misted minds left smoking and crumbling underfoot and staining a country, a faith, a belief spat upon leaving a shattered earth not breathing bodies, not breathing.

A baby died.

Benjamin Carr

FOLLY OF WAR

Many a man has fallen
Through a thing called war
Many a man has fallen
They never knew the score
The big men of power
Kill off the human race
If only they would stop and think
They could save the human race
They send the boys to glory
Or so they tell them so
If only they knew the facts
I don't think anyone would go
To die upon a battlefield
Your life blood flows away
No more to see the sunrise
Or the coming day
Those big men that send them
Just stretch and yawn
They will see the sunrise
And the coming dawn.

John Edney

FORGETTING HER FEELINGS FORGETTING HER TOUCH

She walks barefoot, across the sands
She doesn't care, she's unaware
Of what goes on in the Taliban
Life is free, a food of love
Untouched
By a bloodied glove
Of fear, power and violence

Why mess her around?
Pushing her thoughts underground
Forgetting her feelings
Forgetting her touch
Two paces could change so much
Two paces could change so much

She hides in a veil
I can see her eyes
They're in disguise
Hiding a religion
That kills her passion
For living, for life

Looking at her deep brown eyes
Escaping her dress at Toshmack Place
Nowhere to run, somewhere to hide
Nowhere to run, somewhere to hide
Her life

Aled Hughes

FLY ON THE WALL

Am I invisible to you?
Can you not see my nose,
my two eyes staring,
looking into your soul,
it perplexes me that you see not me,
only your thoughts about,
if I prick my finger I will bleed,
bleed, the scarlet drops on to the dry dirt,
my stomach rumbles with hunger,
my heart aches for you,
you who cannot see me,
you have much life to live,
but my life is done,
and on my white chariot,
riding into the sun,
my bone covered flesh will heal,
I will grow fat,
like you ignoring me,
but I think to myself,
why am I invisible?

Michelle Landon

VE DAY

Today the war in Europe ended,
Humanity sights. It's a tired people
Who celebrate,

The conflict is over,
From many it took everything
From the rest it took more still.

From the homeless, ragged, and the hungry,
Comes the cry, victors we,
Their cries, sound convincing,
Their cries not convincing me.

As the maimed, the broken and
the limbless, struggle to meet the call,
Their story told is visual, while others
Kept in halls, carry wounds
Hard to find, impossible to bind.

Then comes the celebrations,
Troops march, boots and bayonets shine,
Full hearts float on pomp and swagger,
Perhaps a little wine.

As they stand beneath their banners,
Strident bugles claim, victors we,
Their call sounds convincing,
Their call not convincing me.

Alex Laird

VINEGAR AND BROWN PAPER

I have an empty bucket
that I need to return to my neighbour,
who doesn't want to know me.

Shall I throw it over the hedge like a grenade
in an act of devil-may-care defiance?
Or send it on a string between
our bedroom windows like a lifeline?
Or place it gently at her gate as a peace offering?

I can't go *through* her gate -
her weapons of self destruction are contagious.
I need a no man's land and a white flag.

Or this bucket.

I will fill it to brimming with a gift of flowers -
white peaceful flowers
and blue to match her mood
and big sunny yellow ones
to brighten the sky of her despair
and maybe red ones
to show I understand her anger.

She doesn't think I can - but I *do* know
she has been up and up
her personal mountain and tumbled down again
and that she *has* to hit out
and break crowns and friendships.

She said 'I suppose you'll write
a poem about me now.'
No, dear friend and neighbour,
I'm writing a poem *to* you - and it comes
with these flowers and your bucket
full of my best intentions.

Carolyn Garwes

JUST LOOKING ON

Standing here, looking on
I see the pain,
I see the hurt,
But why am I standing here -
    Just looking on?

I don't want to be in the pain,
I don't want to feel the hurt,
So it's safer where I am -
    Just looking on.

Locked inside of me,
There's safety and security
No matter how alone I feel,
But, in the depth of me I know,
It's safer where I am -
    Just looking on.

Yet to those innocent within an ugly war,
The safety's gone and security's defiled,
And loneliness is more acute.
But where are they?
Standing in the midst of it . . .
    Just looking on.

Sue Colson

PEACE

When the dawn came
The bodies lay like fallen flowers
Each hideous in its
Withered array.

The mourners railed
Their cries rending the smoking sky.
Nothing could erase
Their chilled despair.

They fought for this
A barren piece of dusty land.
Their beloved men
Ruled by their dreams.

The dream fulfilled
Gave way to tormented nightmare.
A ransom too much
To give for Peace.

Beryl L Lambert

SOME PEACEFUL ALTERNATIVES

The bayonet in the scabbard
Stained by life's blood red;
A garland of scarlet flower
Worn as a cummerbund instead.

The tapered bullet still breeched
At ready within the gun;
The variances on the wind
Rifling grass in the morning sun.

Unscripted from the heavens
Hate filled letters enveloped in steel;
Lovers beneath Heaven's stars
Caressing words of old appeal.

Echoing sounds from the tramping boots
As the armies march to kill;
The promenade of gentler feet
At the sea shore beyond the hill.

Whosoever sails the mighty seas
Shall fear no oil slick shroud;
Tacking beneath a topsail
Under an ocean blue of cloud.

Hidden devilish diameters
Underground beneath the feet
The land mine where there's gold
Awaiting a wedding ring to greet.

The wail of the anguished parent
At the lamented young-time dead;
The genesis cry at the birth joy,
With longevity at maiden head.

False flashing sunlight cascading,
Its atoms and lepered fall spray
Rains soft fall upon a face,
Upturned in its paternoster to pray.

Peace ends carnage
As at peace carnage begins
Why then carnage peace,
If carnage then peace brings?

Elwyn Johnson

LIVING HUMANITY

What is it that causes despots to rise
all through generations?
The innocent struggle through untold miseries
while demons hold sway.
Their frenetic claws lurk in so many corners,
the goodness of the human race is ever strong
and thinking people of heart hold fast
Look at someone so desperately destroyed
their face ravaged by experience so cruel,
another life taken hostage.
Is it time to put to one side
all the pages of dogma, religion and politics,
restoring humanity to its rightful order?

Margaret Ann Wheatley

LIVING WITH THE ENEMY . . .

As God breathes life into another day,
Your strength rears up to start again,
And as he leaves you with a smile
Your heart is lifted up . . . but then
A phone call wipes the smile away.
The hope is gone, and in its place
A man who's driven by despair,
A man who needs to hear your voice.

Your heart is breaking, yet again,
Oh Lord, give me the will to smile,
To tell him everything is fine,
To reassure him for a while.
With heavy heart, you say goodbye,
You'll see him soon and put things right
You lay the phone down with a sigh
And day has suddenly turned to night.

Sometimes the load's too much to bear,
You feel like running far away,
But you can't leave him to despair,
You have to stay another day.
You know you won't leave him to sink
Into the deep, dark hole that threatens him.
You'll pull him back from the very brink
And love him still . . . will him to win.

Depression haunts the very soul,
It fills the mind to keep it dark.
But to watch it day by day is like
One step forward . . . ten steps back.
You hope each day, with promise new,
That God will wipe away the ache,
And give you both a life that's free
From the scourge that dogs each step you take.

Avril Ann Weryk

IS THERE ANY JUSTICE?

Take a gun, trade it for your mother's life!
Why take us all?
When you only need one!
We mourn for you today, and hope in tomorrow
Comes a better day.
Pig-headed and ignorant, two minds alike!
Take a gun, trade it for your father's life!
Will they ever know what they've started?
Is it for freedom or for peace?
Or sheer American greed?
Even liberation for the Middle East?
Turning you into a self driven money machine.
Rebel. We will! We will!
Take a gun, and trade it for your brother's life!
Be clever. Be wise
See things through our ancestor's eyes.
Watch and you will realise,
Destruction and death is no compromise!
Your hideous excuses for poverty and disease
Why does hatred appear so sane?
Take a gun, trade it for your sister's life!
Disperse the bloodiness from your minds,
Bring to us all, unity, love serenity
Hear our cry!
We don't want to die!
Just listen to us cry,
Our world doesn't deserve to die!
Take a gun, trade it for your son's life!
Listen now to the people's voices
Replace our fears and mistrusts
With piece of mind.

In every land beyond the eye,
No religion. No creed. No race,
Deserves such hate and disgrace.
Take a gun and trade it for your daughter's life!
Come together, unite as one,
Be strong, become whole and do the right thing!
Our world is dying, because of your war!
Have you no sorrow, guilt or even shame?
Truth is greater than your ego's army,
Mother Nature, world creator!
Hear the people's cry,
Listen carefully, listen
Hear the people's cry,
But why? But why?

Ally Joyner & Andy McLaughlin

Railway Station In War

On platform one, a milling throng
Navy, khaki and Air Force blue
Snatches of some old marching song;
Steaming locomotive reverses in
To head departing troop train.
Mothers, wives, children, lovers
Even some dads and brothers.
Whistles blow, slamming doors,
Clouding steam up front,
Waving, smiles, wet with tears
Faces showing fears.

But, across on platform four
Another darkened train
Slips silently in
No wives, no lovers wait
Just nurses wearing crosses red.

Arthur J Pullen

A NATION MOURNS

A nation mourns
Our eyes with unshed tears burn
As sounds of war around us fall
And memories half-forgotten, now return

A nation mourned
When mothers saw sons and loved ones off to war
Now! The sons of those same sons
Face an enemy once more.

A nation mourns,
When one such son on to foreign soil falls
So young - too young
For them the 'Last Post' calls.

A nation mourns
To know no words of comfort spoken
Can heal those hearts so swiftly broken
A nation mourns.

C Worthington

ERASED

Only the crows were told of their passing
No military markers show the spot
No cross, no crescent
No mellowed ivy-draped memorial
Where comrades may lay wreaths in autumn
As the days lengthen, only in some hearts
There moves the grief which dare not weep aloud
They fought for the right but the right became the wrong
They were on the other side

M C Tshiamalenge

A TIME FOR WAR?
(A father recalls the death of his son)

They gave my boy a gun
and sent him off to war,
'We'll make a man of you,' they said.
'It's war my boy, it's war!'

They gave him a smart new uniform
and shiny boots to wear,
they taught him to fight and kill,
to die in a manly way!
'Your king and country need you!'
Was the slogan of the day . . .
His young life was ended
in a morass of mud and clay.

He lies at peace in a foreign field
a thousand poppies above his head,
a lark serenades him sweetly
Mother Earth provides his bed.

Now the memories come flooding back
of a small boy, happy at play
joyfully laughing and shouting,
greeting each new day.

They gave my boy a gun
and sent him off to war,
'We'll make a man of you!' they said . . .
'It's war, my boy, it's war!'

Arthur Pickles

WAR

I read, I read
Your words with sorrow
With anger, anger
But what does that do?
How does that help?
I realise how lucky I am
To be safe
With everything I need
Yet you
You have nothing
Nothing but hope
Hope that your family will not feel much pain
Hope that it will soon come to an end
Stop
Stop the killing, torturing
But when will that happen?
When?
Maybe tomorrow
Maybe never
But I will end
With these last words
I hold hope
Hope that one day
A stop, to the unlawful beating
We live in hope
For you, us, everyone
Peace.

Jodie Booth (14)

BEWARE OF WAR

Can there be any justification for war
Misery, slaughter, destroying, the death of nations.
War is even glorified in the Bible
And some of the hymns we sing
We are only here for a little while
So why destroy one another at will
With indescribable weapons of destruction
War deprived me of my youth and freedom
And of knowing one of my grandfathers
Who died of wounds, the year I was born
I will never forgive the politicians and dictators
For allowing the things to happen
The whole world should gang up to stop
Any country who threatens peace
They used to call the British Army lions led by donkeys
I remember the Territorial Army (Terriers) on parade
A fine body of men going away to the war
Most of them finished up a mark on the Cenotaph
When I think of the millions who have died at war
And the innocents who never harmed a soul
You wonder what the hell is wrong with this world
What chance have we got of peace
When we are all different colours
Talk different languages, with different religions
The only thing that will unify this world
Will be an invasion from outer space
But I doubt if that will ever happen
If they have any sense they will steer clear of us
So we will keep our fingers crossed
That our men of wisdom will do the right thing
And someday there will be peace on earth.

James Rodger

HOMECOMING

My daddy is gone from home
My daddy has gone to war
He sailed off in a ship to a 'Hip-hip-hip!'
My daddy is gone from home.

My daddy has gone to war
My daddy has sailed to the east
He'd right on his side and a good spring tide
My daddy has gone to war.

My daddy has gone to the east
My daddy has sailed away
There's no news of him and the omens are grim
My daddy has gone to the east.

My daddy has sailed away
My daddy is far from home
I'm playing it cool, just bobbing off school
For my daddy has sailed away.

My daddy is far from home
My daddy just up and left
But mum's in a funk and her friend's done a bunk
For Daddy is coming home!

Harold Wonham

THE SOLDIER

They put a rifle in my hand
And taught me how to shoot
How to aim and fire and kill
How to black my boots
With a pack upon my back
I slog through muddy lanes
Up and over mountains
Run through pouring rain
Keep your head up, shoulders back
What's it all about?
March in time and swing your arms
Eyes right, eyes left - salute!
They say now I'm a soldier
I must go out and fight
I must kill my enemies
They say that it's all right
Now I am a hero
The war is over now
Lay down your arms - forget it
But they don't tell me how!
They've trained me as a soldier
I've watched people die
They taught me how to kill and maim
They didn't tell me *why?*

Lydia Barnett

THE GIRL WHO KEPT CRYING

Upon this winter's earth
the corpse of summer lies.
The girl cries a tear
for the white rose
and the lost.
Fidgets briefly with her glasses,
then sighs and looks out
upon the nothingness
and dreams a dreamless
nightmare of remembrance
and cries once more.

Michael Wilson

THE CONCENTRATION CAMP

When the gates were opened
And they saw what was inside
The bravest of brave
Just bowed their heads and cried
The stench of human bodies
The skeletons called men
A thousand score lay on the ground
A thousand score and ten
Their mouths and tongues all swollen
Their eyes so sunk and dim
Their camp clothes torn and filthy
A cover for frail bodies within
They suffered starvation and torture
They saw their real friends die
They dug the open graves for them
But for them they could not cry
This was a camp built on hatred
For people in deepest despair
But for them when the gates were opened
Thanked God
With clasped hands and a prayer

Ivor Percival

POPPY DAY

November the 11th, a day we remember
those who fought the war
and suffered violence, blood and gore
men who were so very brave
could only watch as their friends fell to the grave

Some are still here,
some gave their lives,
let's thank those brave men
who brought peace to our lives

May we remember to pray to God
for peace each day
for this is the way our world must stay.

Elliot Liversey (11)

ISLANDS

Earth islands and continents
Lie in seas of discontent,
As man forever seeks to change
His own environment.

Tides of envy, hatred, despair and greed
Wash high upon the shores,
Leaving countless drowning in the wake
Of worthless projects, endless wars.

Following slogan, chant, or battle cry,
Hope or fervour in his eyes,
Man steps onto uncharted paths,
Oft leading to his own demise.

He unlocks natures every door,
Dissecting, changing all he sees;
Ignoring the cost of each intrusion;
And nature will extract her fees.

Be he scientist, soldier, sinner, saint,
Man will ever turn his gaze away
From nature's multi-million years,
And the world is changed, in one short stay.

Mans' arrogance, his intolerance,
Will haste the ending of the human race,
And God's tears will fall on island earth
Circling silently in space.

Thomas R Slater

1939-P45 (THE GREAT DOOR)

We are coming home to England
that's our next address,
where there's freedom of the press.
We are coming home to England
if England there be
and there to plant our family tree.
We are coming home to England
at half past three,
be sure to put the kettle on
we'll be ready for some tea.
We are coming home to England
because we've found the map
the cat sat on, to guide us across the sea.
But never having been here before
and not wishing to declare war,
please welcome us to your shore,
please, please don't close the door.
It's in your law to help the poor,
more and more and more.
That's the ticket,
our poverty, we'll kick it,
together we'll lick it.

Vann Scytere

FOR THOSE WHO CAME HOME

Soft, the hail, like a cloud's confetti.
Soft, the snow, like angel's feathers.
Soft, the seasons, held in happiness.
Never hinting at the blizzards to come.
Never hinting at an avalanche's fall.
All the while the wind howls it's battle chants,
enough to sear the blood of innocents.

Back across a river of blood stains,
striding back with our eyes aloft.
No surrender, hand or heart.
No surrender, mind or spirit.
Honour be ours, forever after,
honour all the age should know.

Soft, the wind, like a children's choir.
Soft, the rain, like Heaven's tears.
Soft, the years, remembered in gladness.
Never hinting at the storms to come.
Never hinting at a whirlwind's passage.
All the while the clouds clap their thunder,
enough to tear our hearts asunder.

Back across the blackened and sooted roads,
marching back with heads held high.
No surrender, home or heritage.
No surrender, memory or soul.
Honour be ours, forever after,
honour all the age should know.

(Nature's peace is the Earth,
to whom we owe our birth.
Made from dust and returned to dust,
one thing that it holds is our trust . . .)

Dale Mullock

THE HARVEST OF CONFLICT

Seeds!
Of future generations
Trodden in the ground
Germination!
Buried deep and
Fertilised by blood
Intention!
Greed - Power - Hatred
Victory - in futile strife
Harvest!
The fallen fruit
Of a Mother's womb
Success!
No crop here - will
Grow and prosper
Death!
The only peace
On this killing field
Result!
No one wins - just
Waste - and carnage of our fellow man!

Olga Margaret Moorhouse

PLEASE STOP!

Upon the ravaged earth, we all depend on oil,
The safety in our lives, yet the world that we spoil,
Rests in the hands of madmen, of the Bush and the Blair,
From America, the only law, unto themselves,
Will condemn thousands more to the oil fires they'll dare

The martial might flexes, the wounded land of the free.
Makes ready, to secure its investments, its righteous killing spree.
The monsters we spawn, evolve from a fuel thirsty state,
To arm and destroy, the puppet, the tyrant, the cycle of hate.

Who are the demons, in the call to arms,
Bullets for the hungry, no food from the farms,
Exports of heroin, for western addictions,
Fair trade dreamers, lost summit convictions.
An Islamic jihad, murder the west, and to starve it from oil,
Lets rubble and raise them, their evils to foil.

Perhaps one day, when the oil runs dry,
We'll pray to the elements, 'It's peace,' we'll cry,
Then we'll win, our rights to all the weather,
And destroy our foes again, forever and ever!

Just a dream, to stop the killing,
Peace on Earth, America, a thought so chilling.
I may be misguided to think this way,
Is might always right from the US of A.
It is my sadness that my dreams may be wrong,
To loathe injustice and conflict, through a poem and song.

So to you Burning Bush and the Bewitchment of Blair,
To arms, to war, and butcherous slaughter.
Your path is all open - Iraq's over there!

Philip Lowe

WHO ARE THE DEAD

At the going down of the sun we shall remember them

The author of these words may well be dead
And wrote in vain.
A new generation comes along and in their name
One asks the question
Who are the dead we must all keep in recollection?
Why did they die? And for whose sake
Did they give up the gift of life and deaths dark pathway take?
The years have set their sacrifice at nought
Where is the peace their lives so dearly bought?
The flame of their offering died as quick as they
A new generation rises, *kneel and pray.*

D Adams

TOMORROW?

Today there is no sound, only a deathly silence, in contrast to yesterdays artillery barrage, of so long.
Around me, only the flies buzz, the sound magnified by the solitude, as I lie on my belly, 'watching my front'.

Suddenly, on a nearby twig, I see another figure, a solitary robin, with his little brown coat, and its red splash on his breast.
I watch him, and enjoy his company. He watches me, chirping cheekily, he has no fear of me, why should he?
Suddenly there is more movement, as five more figures come into view, they are dressed in field grey.

One is bigger than the others, and slower in his movements. My left hand tightens on the rifle barrel, as my index finger runs along the trigger guard. 'Eyes line up the sights, restrain the breathing, take the first pressure, do not dwell in the aim'. 'Take the second pressure'. The crack of the rifle breaks the silence, and my little friend takes flight in alarm. 200 yards away, the largest figure jerks upright, and I see the red stain on his breast, rather like that of my little feathered friend. I see the man's comrades dive for cover. My little friend will be far away by now, and I too must go, while I still can. Perhaps I will see him again tomorrow, if there is a tomorrow . . .

D K Brough

REMEMBRANCE

Remember, remember
the remembrance of men
who fought for our freedom
with loyalty and sin.

Their courage unbroken.
Their senses alert.
With no real idea
the impact they'd convert.

The boldness of our heroes
shall never lie in the dust.
Our poppy parades
shall make sure of their just.

Vicki Watson

THE AMERICAN CEMETERY, CAMBRIDGE

In grounds donated by the University, the dead lie silent.
Bodies drawn from the battlefields of Europe:
North America, France, the waters of the Atlantic,
now rest in thirty acres of arcing rows,
gleaming white and standing to attention; predictable as horoscopes.

As spots go, this is Elgar and Wordsworth:
unbroken green, save for the occasional Norman church
carefully placed like a chess piece
between the squares of hedge and field;
Ely Cathedral, 14 miles hence,
visible only on a clear day.

Woods skirt the west and south roads,
threatening leafy invasions of Japanese pagoda,
firethorn and forsythia; an edgy Burnam burgeoning
adolescent fruit, still anxious on the bough.

Around the memorial chapel of portland stone,
nobody speaks. The breeze beats softly
upon its teak entrance, laden with bronze and thick
as cathedral doors. The tanks and landing craft
beaten into its design are green with six decades
of English rain.

Inside, the map of the Air Assault on Axis Europe
is littered with flags and criss-crossed,
like flight routes illustrated in duty free packed in-flight magazines.
All around are the glass cases that hold the Bronze Stars,
Legions of Merit and Purple Hearts of the fallen -
set in lonely isolation, like the lava-casts of the contorted dead
in similar cases at Pompeii.

Andrew Detheridge

OUR FAITHERS WHA FAUGHT AFORE US

That auld enemy tried tae rid oor nation
but back tae Englin they did flee,
when Wallace in his heelin might
faught fir Scoatlin's liberty.

Their magistrates tried tae breed us oot
raping young brides oan the nights they wed,
strippin thum o their innocence
oan their matrimonial beds.

Ootnumberin wild celtic warriors
by mair than four tae one,
their king sat high upoan his hoarse
as the battle had begun.

Oan his armies Longshanks turned his back
he fled south frae oor heathurd glens,
leavin there ahent him
twinty thousin deein men.

The English came again
bit they came again too soon,
against The Bruce at Bannockburn
oan the twinty-fourth o June.

That day his long since gone
and once again, Scoatlin's free,
risin strong as a nation
wie pride and liberty.

We'll wear oor kilts wie honour
oor pipes'll chant in chorus,
bowin doon tae nae-one
rememberin oor faithers wha faught afore us.

Michael McLellan

WAR HAS NO WINNERS

When will man ever learn?
What wisdom needed to discern?
No killing is above the law,
No winners in any war.

We won't put up with their threats,
We'll kill the enemy with our jets,
Top brass to control the press,
Tell the truth more or less.

Collateral Damage is what they call it;
Don't like to say what caused it.
Innocent people blown to pieces,
Don't mention this in press releases.

It seems we never learn from history,
Finding a peaceful solution still a mystery.
We live the lie of 'war and glory'.
War has no winners, is the truthful story.

Simon Icke

THE FIELDS OF FLANDERS

When I close my eyes
I can see the field of Flanders
Poppies bold red swaying to and fro
For they are the blood of the brave
For each life a poppy appears
It was so many, they will grow
For many more years
Loved ones lost on battlefields
Far away from home
If they were here I know they'd say
Could it have been done another way?
Peace came at such a price
To witness horrors all around
As men lay dying some made no sound
Alone in mud in the ground
Others cried, shouted out in pain
Please God take me in your arms
Love me, hold me tight
Its gone so dark and I'm afraid
I'll not make it through the night
Men made their peace
Many prayers quietly said
Lying in mud no comfort bed
Minds full of thoughts
Of loved ones far away
Close to their hearts
Many tears were shed
Comrades said their sad farewells
Gave comfort where they stood
Do not forget us when we are gone
Remember it was done for you
When peace comes let there be no more wars

For they must cease
Learn to love and to share
Live in peacetime everywhere
Holding hands stand firm together
For we will not be far away
Many brave men died this day
To set our country free
And when you see those poppies tall
One of them is me.

Valerie Anderson

AT THE FEET OF STRAND 22

Pigs of the G-war
Nauseate from afar
The precarious state of mind
Of the terminally unkind
Infect the aura
Of our flora

The future of mice and men
Laid, extracted, modified
To a zombie nation
Equality in a far flung nebular

Seen by this king
In a prophetic vision
Synthesised in my DNA
Tells of our need to create
Which is our need to destroy
Yet we need to baby-sit, not destroy
The eroticism of our minds
Less we become our destiny

Christopher David

SUBMISSIONS INVITED
SOMETHING FOR EVERYONE

POETRY NOW 2003 - Any subject, any style, any time.

WOMENSWORDS 2003 - Strictly women, have your say the female way!

STRONGWORDS 2003 - Warning! Opinionated and have strong views. (Not for the faint-hearted)

All poems no longer than 30 lines.
Always welcome! No fee!
Cash Prizes to be won!

Mark your envelope (eg *Poetry Now*) *2003*
Send to:
Forward Press Ltd
Remus House, Coltsfoot Drive,
Peterborough, PE2 9JX

OVER £10,000 POETRY PRIZES TO BE WON!

Judging will take place in October 2003